GRADE AA Approved

Tells Tall Tales

Will Work for Chicken Feed

Just Roosting, Thanks.

Question THANKSGIVING

HUMPTY DUMPTY is a FALL GUY!

THE WORLD'S GREATEST BOOK OF CHICKEN JOKES

CHICKEN JOKES

And Other Fowl Humor

The World's Greatest Book of
CHICKEN JOKES
And Other Fowl Humor

By
Sol Morrison

Illustrations
by
Walt Hopmans

JESTER BOOKS
Imprint of The Poetry Center Press

Published by The Poetry Center Press, Orinda, California

International Standard Book Number: 0-940861-57-7

JESTER BOOKS

Imprint of *The Poetry Center Press*

Division of Shoestring Press, Orinda, California 94563
Book Design: Philip Morrison

Table of Contents

Introduction

The Classic Joke: *"Why did the chicken cross the road?"*
The Classic Answer: *"To get to the other side."*

From earliest times, our ancestors hungered for and endlessly pursued two vital needs: food and knowledge. (Fresh air and water were taken for granted back then—who knew?)

So after filling up on *Pteroduckt yl a l'Orange* and *Blackened Fowlasaurus*, they turned their attention towards knowledge and in short order invented a mind-stretching game they called: THE QUESTION.

It was very popular and soon every possible question was answered except two: 1. *"Which came first, the Dinosaur or the Egg"*,
2. *"Why did the Dinosaur cross the road?"*

After several million years of trying to find good answers the Dinosaurs packed up and moved on. The un-answered questions, however, stayed with us though they have evolved through the ages:

1. *"Which came first, the Chicken or the Egg?"*
2. *"Why did the Chicken cross the road?"*

The best answer I ever heard to the first riddle came from a young TV Show Contestant: "The chicken came first", he said, "because God wouldn't lay an egg."

The solution to the other question: 'to get to the other side' is both simple and logical.

And now since we finally do have good answers to these pre-historic questions, that should be the end of the Chicken Jokes, right?

Funny you should ask. . .

□□□□□□□□□□

HINTS ON WRITING YOUR OWN BOOK OF CHICKEN JOKES.

Start with the basic "road riddle" formula: "Why did the (fill-in) cross the (fill-in)?" Then try some variations. Remember, if it's okay for supermarkets to sell bologna made from chicken and burgers made from turkey, then you can feel free to include "bologna chicken" jokes..."lion chicken" jokes...even "people chicken" jokes. Anything capable of crossing a road is fair game.

Note: Please do not send me any chicken Jokes;
I already have more than enough for a second book!

Preface

How this book got hatched...

First, I want to say that I never intended to do a whole book of chicken jokes. It all started at a family get-together when I casually mentioned finding an old notebook of mine filled with humorous variations explaining why chickens and other fowl creatures obsessively crossed the road.

"Chicken Jokes?" My older brother Phil asked.

"Left over from *Laugh-in Magazine*. Remember, I wrote one-liners for them?"

"H-m-m-m-m."

"Must be 200 jokes in that old notebook," I said.

"Well, Sol," Phil said, just making conversation, "if you can come up with a thousand jokes, I'll publish a Chicken Joke Book."

And so I did.

About the Author :

Sol Morrison has been writing since high school. First, as a copywriter with department stores and advertising agencies and later, freelance. His jokes and humorous material have been published in magazines and newspapers and performed on radio and television. Sol occasionally performs stand-up comedy at local clubs. By Official Proclamation the Mayor and City Council of Santa Barbara have named Sol the Honorary Town Jester in recognition of his light-hearted reflections about his home town. He lives with his wife, two daughters and two cats in Santa Barbara, California.

About the Illustrator:

Walt Hopmans is both an artist and writer of prose, poetry and humor. He has also written and directed shows for local theater. Retired from the teaching profession, Walt is director of the Santa Barbara Writers Consortium and is active in numerous art and civic programs. He lives with his wife Alice, in Santa Barbara.

Acknowledgements

Walt Hopmans—Good friend and talented artist, who created the cartoons and illustrated the jokes with imagination and wit. He also contributed many original ideas and proved to be an agreeable traveling companion through all the twists, turns and detours we made crossing this road together.

Philip Morrison—My editor and publisher, who slogged through hundreds of disjointed chicken parts with reasonable equanimity and unexplainable good humor. "Thanks, Phil for not chickening-out on that wonderfully rash offer to publish my book. Hey, what's a brother for?"

Shirley Morrison—My patient wife who suffered through many a trial balloon–never letting the occasional lead one flatten her support and encouragement. And to daughters Nina and Toby for the enthusiastic way they kept asking when the book would be finished—so they could share it with friends.

My thanks to you all,

Sol D. Morrison

SECTION 1
CHICKEN BEHAVIOR:
a look at motivational influences

"TO BE, OR NOT TO BE..."

Why did the chicken cross the baseball field?
To get the other side out.

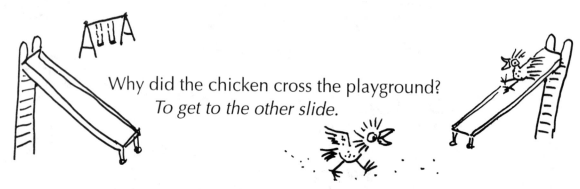

Why did the chicken cross the playground?
To get to the other slide.

Why did the chicken cross the amusement park?
To get to the other ride.

Why did the chicken cross the nesselrode?
To get to the other side dish.

Why did the chicken cross Rhodesia?
To get to the other tide.

Why did the chicken cross the dining room?
To get to the other side board.

Why did the chicken cross the apple orchard?
To get to the other cider.

Why did the chicken cross the town square?
He just didn't want to go a-round.

Why did the chicken cross India?
To get to the other Sahib.

Why did the chicken cross the Gossip Magazine's editorial room?
To get to the other snide.

When did the chicken cross the bridge?
When he came to it, of course!

Why did the chicken cross the room full of uppity people?
To get to the other snobs.

Why did the chicken cross the Navy pier?
To get to the other sub.

When is chicken soup bad for your health?
When you're the chicken, of course!

What did the turkey do after refusing to cross the busy street?
He ducked the issue by chickening out.

What did Chicken Little do with the duck tape?
He held a wrap session.

When did the chicken duck out of Turkey?
When the Squab Mob tried to cook her goose.

How does a young chicken get around in a hurry?
As a frequent fryer.

Where did chickens first start crossing the road?
In the state of Road Island.

How did the farmer get the chicken across the road?
He was forced to pullet.

Why did the religious chicken cross Israel?
To get to the other Zion.

What do chickens use to catch fish?
> *Fishing cackle.*

When was Chicken Little sent to the showers?
> *When she fowled out.*

What did the poor farmer do when his Hen House burned down?
> *He used the insurance money to re-coop.*

Why did the rooster cross the railroad tracks?
> *It was just a spur of the moment decision.*

When was the chicken arrested?
> *When she ran a-fowl of the law.*

Why did the stewed chicken cross the road?
> *To get to the A.A. Meeting.*

How does a chicken earn the right to be in a Chicken Pot Pie?
She has to get potted, of course.

Why was the fowl farmer forger arrested?
His rubber chick bounced.

How did the chicken cope when she came to a busy road?
She plucked up her courage and winged it.

Why did the rooster smash down the theater door?
He wanted to break into "crow business."

Why did the chicken cross the River Jordan?
To get to the "milk and honey" on the other side.

Why did the chicken cross the drawbridge?
Ambition. She longed to move people with her drawings.

10 Answers To The Burning Question: Why Did The Chicken Double-Cross The Road:

10. The road turned against her.

9. She wanted to make it "a road *more* travelled."

8. She was into cross-training.

7. She was searching for a public roost-room.

6. She was a hair-brained chick with split ends.

5. The road threw her a curve.

4. Nostalgic, she wanted to re-trace her steps.

3. She was trying to cement their relationship.

2. Because the road had done her dirt.

1. It was an ex-Spearment. . .to "double her pleasure."

Pick a Punch Line:

☐ I think we picked the wrong place in line.
☐ Can I see the Cruise Reservations again?
☐ It can't start raining soon enough for me!
☐ I hope there's lots of food on board.
☐ What I said was: "Let's get in front
of the <u>line</u>. Not the <u>Lion</u>!"
☐ Maybe those UNICORNS had the right
idea after all!

Did the rubber chicken have trouble getting across the road?
Yes indeed–it was quite a stretch.

What happened when the rubber chicken ran afoul of the law?
They sent him up for a long stretch.

What does a rubber chicken get after laying eggs for 5 years?
Highly visible STRETCH MARKS!

Why did the rubber chicken cross the road?
She wanted to stretch her legs.

How did the rubber chicken cross the basketball court?
She was dribbled across.

Shell Shocked!

Does a chicken wishbone always bring good luck?
Not to the chicken!

Why did the chicken plucker cross the road?
To celebrate Feather's Day.

Why did the feather cross the road?
The answer is blowing in the wind.

Why did the feather bed manufacturer cross the road?
To get to the other chickens.

Why did Jack Frost refuse to cross the windy road?
He was a draft dodger.

What talisman should a chicken-inspector carry?
A good pluck charm.

What does the farmer say to his hens after feeding them?
"Have a nice lay."

FRYER-WORKS IN THE HEN YARD

* This is the road
LES traveled.

This is "LES".

What is better than chicken a la king?
A commoner in the barnyard.

Why do ducks waddle?
Waddle you give me if I tell you?

How did the chicken leave the fowl ball?
She ducked out.

What do you call a chicken with dreadlocks who plays reggae music?
A Roosterfarian.

What do city slickers call chickens who live in the sticks?
Yolk-els.

Do Roosters have teeth?
Yes of course--in their comb.

Define a journeyman Rooster:
A pro crow.

Name of a "low-life" bar for fowls:
"The Swan Dive."

Early Morning "Work-up Calls"

These days everybody has to specialize, even Roosters.

How Many Rooster Crow-calls Can You Match Up?

A. Matchmaker	1. DOC-a-doodle-do
B. Preacher	2. Cock-a-POODLE-do
C. Locksmith	3. CRICK-a-doodle-do
D. Classical Pianist	4. CREEK-a-doodle-do
E. Chef	5. Cock-a-doodle-do-UNTO-OTHERS
F. Oriental Cook	6. DOCK-a-doodle-do
G. Chiropractor	7. Cock-a-doodle-MOO
H. Dog-walker	8. Cock-a-doodle-GNU
I. Pawnshop Helper	9. Cock-a-doodle-SUE
J. Longshoreman	10. Cock-a-doodle-SIOUX
K. Potter	11. Cock-a-doodle-STEW
L. Swim Coach	12. Cock-a-doodle-WOO
M. Sheepherder	13. Cock-a-doodle-EWE
N. Gossip Columnist	14. BACH-a-doodle-do
O. Pop Musician	15. ROCK-a-doodle-do
P. Short Order Cook	16. WOK-a-doodle-do
Q. Athlete	17. YOK-a-doodle-do
R. Native American Tribe Member	18. YACKETY-YAK-a-doodle-do
S. Zoo Keeper	19. HOCK-a-doodle-do
T. Clothes Designer	20. HAM—a-doodle-do
U. Milkman	21. CLOCK-a-doodle-do
V. Lawyer	22. FROCK-a-doodle-do
W. Medical person	23. JACK-a-doodle-do
X. Stand-up Comic	24. LOCK-a-doodle-do
Y. Brewer	25. BOCK-a-doodle-do
Z. Watchmaker	26. CROCK-a-doodle-do

"*A Chicken in the hand, is worth two in the store.*"

"The Ugly Duckling" is a beautiful story.

"The chick is in the mail."

"Never stick your neck out... unless you're a swan."

What did the French Chef say?
Parley vous chicken stew?

Why did the Hawk cross the road?
To get the other chicken.

Why did the robber chicken cross the gangster's hideout?
To get to the other bribe.

Why did the ice-skating chicken cross the rink?
To get to the other glide.

When did the dynamite tester cross the road?
Approximately 10 seconds after he lit the fuse.

Why did the rabbit in the tuxedo dash across the busy road?
He was late for the Hare Ball.

What did the rabbit do to get across the train yard?
He hopped a freight.

Why did the clown cross the carnival grounds?
To get to the other side show.

How did the chicken get across the railroad yard?
She was railroaded.

How did the rabbit manage to get across the busy restaurant?
He table hopped. (With Sandra and the Maitré de).

Why did Basil and Rosemary cross the road?
They needed Thyme to add a little spice to their lives.

Why did the chicken cross the Rubicon?
To get to the other Caesar salad.

Why did B'rer Rabbit cross the road??
He had a briar engagement.

What do the wild geese do when they can't get across the road?
They Honker Down and wait in the Honky Tonk.

Why did the crop duster cross the road?
To get another dust rag.

Why did the chicken run across the road?
He wanted to jog his memory.

Why did the goose depart the monastery?
He was de-flocked.

What happened when the chicken crossed the trampoline?
She hit the ceiling.

Which came first, the chicken or the road?
The egg.

Why did the chicken cross the theater?
He was just going through a stage.

A BOOBY HATCH

What did the chicken do on finding herself in lots of hot water?
> *She got all steamed up.*
> *or...She just sat and stewed. (Hey, why sweat it?)*
> *or...She wanted to fricasee what would happen.*

Special drink for chickens during time their feathers fall out:
> *Chocolate Moult.*

Where do hens now live?
> *In the great state of Hens-sylvania.*

And where did hens used to live?
> *Must have been pre-Hensylvania.*

Why did the mud hen come back across the road?
> *She was a dirty double-crosser!*

Why did the roosters go on strike?
> *They were tired of working for chicken feed.*

What do you call a henhouse celebration where they make fun of the guest of honor?
> *A Roost Roast.*

Why did the lawyer cross the courtroom?
> *To get the other side.*

How did the rooster cross the road?
> *In a roadster.*

Why did the rich chicken cross the stormy dirt road?
> *To deposit her nest egg in the mud bank.*

Why did the chicken hurry past the IBM building?
> *She didn't want to get stuck in computer traffic.*

Why did the chicken cross The Great Barrier Reef?
> *For no reason a-toll.*

Why did the amoeba cross the road?
It was time to split.

What do you get if you cross the road with a chicken?
A book like this one.

What do you get if you cross a deadend street with a duck?
A cul de quack.

Where did the dancing cow cross the road?
At Hoof-er Dam.

Where do birds cross the road?
At the Tern pike.

When do birds cross the road?
During thrush hour.

What happens when the baby chicks come home to roost?
Parents lose their game room...and the food bill goes up.

By Their Crows Shall Ye Know Them.

Cock-A-Dawdle-Do: Procrastinating Rooster.

Creak-A-Doodle-Do: Elderly Rooster's Crow.

Croak-A-Doodle-D0: Rooster at a Funeral.

Cooker-Doodle-Do: Rooster Chef.

Kick-A-Doodle-Do: Dancing Rooster.

Wise-Crack-A-Doodle-Do: Comedian Rooster.

Cock-A-Deedle-Deedle-Do: Israeli Rooster's crow.

Crook-A-Doodle-Do: Dishonest Rooster.

Mock-A-Doodle-Do: Fake Rooster

Doc-A-Doodle-Do: Medical Rooster

Cock-a-Mamie Do: Weird Rooster's Crow.

How does a blue-eyed crooner Rooster greet the dawn?
   "Cock-a-doodle-Do-Be-Do-Be-Do."

What does the contrary Rooster say each dawn?
   COCK-A-DOODLE-DON'T.

To keep his wake-up job, the Union Rooster must pay...
   Cock-A-Doodle Dues.

Amish Quackers:
    "Fine Feathered Friends".

Why did the Goose Grease cross the road?
    To get to Skid Row.

When did the Goose cross the road?
    Only after the Goose got Loooose.

Exactly when did Zorro's friends know he was chicken?
    When he put his capon.

Why didn't the chicken cross the English Channel?
She refused to go through channels.

How did the wealthy rubber chicken cross the road?
In her Cadillac stretch limo.

Which came first: the chicken joke or the egg?
The salt.

How did the egg salad cross the road?
He was on a roll.

Why did the mock turtle cross the road?
It was just to "mock" you.

Why did the mock turtle pretend to cross the road?
To get a part in this joke book!

Multiple Choice Question:
Why did the Chicken Pie cross the road?
BECAUSE...
A. She was in a Pie-athalon.
B. She was pie-eyed.
C. She was fit to be pied, or,
D. She was playing pied and seek.

Poetic Justice

Why did the chicken cross the farm?
To get to the other silo.

Why did the chicken cross the horse breeder's ranch?
To get to the other sire.

Why did the chicken cross the pharmacy?
To get to the other salve.

Why did the chicken cross the Everglades Swamp?
To get to the other Cypress.

Why did the chicken cross lover's lane?
To get to the other sigh.

Why did the chicken cross the Swedish car lot?
To get to the other Saab.

Why did the chicken cross the movie studio lot?
To get to the other scene.

Why did the chicken cross the Weight Watcher Salon?
To get to the other sag.

Why did the Rooster criss-cross the sandy beach?
He was searching for his comb.

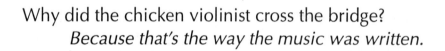

Why did the chicken cross the airport?
He felt flighty.

Why did the chicken violinist cross the bridge?
Because that's the way the music was written.

Why did the chicken weave across the road?
Because he was a basket case.

Why did the depressed chicken cross the road?
To get to the other sigh.

What do pyschiatrists eat for dinner when in a fowl mood?
De-Pressed Duck.

How do you transport fowl to market?
Inside a cluck-truck.

Appropriate dessert for a Rooster's Birthday:
Cake-A-Doodle-Do!

Ethnic Poultry

IRE-ISH   SWEET-ISH   FIN-ISH

Why didn't Dorothy Lamour cross the Road to Zanzibar?
Bing told her it was the sarong thing to do.

(So, ask your grandparents.)

HONEST CAL CAPON'S FINE USED CARS

➡ *Chev-ro-lay*
➡ *Cackle-lac*
➡ *Toy-yolk-a*
➡ Hen-da
➡ Stewed E. Baker
➡ L-egg-sus
➡ Mercedes-Hens

Plus: Hatch-Backs,

Chicken Coupés

& Cabrio-Lays

Why did the chicken need a guide to cross Switzerland?
He couldn't Alp himself.

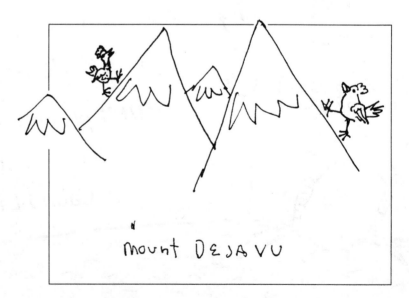

Why did the chicken cross the Swiss Alps twice?
He wanted a second Alping.

Famous Sayings Chickens Live By

—"A rolling chicken gathers no feathers."

—"A chicken in the hand is worth two in the hen house."

—"All that glitters is not chicken feed."

—"Pluck Feathers in haste; Eat chicken in leisure."

—"Sticks and stones may break my bones,
   but at least chicken soup will make me feel better."

—"A stitch in time, holds in the turkey stuffing."

—"A chicken a day keeps the butcher in business."

—"A bowl of chicken soup a day keeps the Doctor away."

—"Feed a chicken, starve a cold Duck."

—"Chicken out in haste, live to fight another day."

—"Hatch Chickens — Not plots."

—"Don't count your chicken wires before they're patched."

How did the chicken cross the bedroom?
She went undercover.

Why did the chicken cross the subway?
She was feeling under the weather.

Why did the chicken cross the Carnival?
To get to the other side-show.

Why did the lazy chicken cross the road?
It was the very least she could do.

Why did the chicken cross the road in a hot air balloon?
a. She wanted to keep her trip above board,
b. She was having high level talks,
c. She was flying high, or
d. She wanted to keep her spirits up.

Reader's
Choice:

New Movies Coming To Your Local Theater

CROW MAGNON: Pre-historic Rooster

As Featured in the book:
Dr. Cackle & Mr. Fried.

Where did the dancing chicken cross the road?
When she came to the STEP sign.

How do chickens make love?
In a prescribed pecking ardor.

When do Roosters brood?
When they are hen-pecked.

How do chickens select their leader?
By a show of hens.

How can you recognize a duck crossing?
By all of the quacks in the pavement.

When do vacationing hens take a travel break?
When they come to a "nest stop" along the road.

When does a Rooster cross the road?
In good feather weather.
(Because he is weather vain.)

Why did the plucked-nude chicken cross the restaurant kitchen?
She was hired to pop out of the saucy chicken pie at a stag party.

Let's Hear it for Every Chicken's Favorite Comedian:

HEN-NY YOUNGMAN

Why did Hen-ny Youngman cross the road?
To get to the other chicken joke.

When did the chicken run across the road?
When Hen-ny Youngman ran out of good jokes.

Why did the chicken cross the road?
To get away from Hen-ny Youngman.

What famous musical is about Hen-ny 's life?
"The Bantam of The Opera."

Why does Hen-ny wear Rhode Island RED Suspenders?
To take the slack out of his comedy routines.

Why did Hen-ny slowly walk across the road ?
He's just not the Young-man he used to be.

Quid Pro Crow: *Youngman fiddles while George Burns.*

CHICKEN⊗
(population, 37)

ALASKA

A Salute to CHICKEN, ALASKA
Wherever you may wander, there's no place like Nome...

Why did the frozen chicken cross the Alaskan Highway?
He thaw a better life on the other side.

How did the frozen chicken cross the road?
He rode his ice-cycle.

Why did the Ptarmigan cross the road?
Ptarm Marches On!

Why did the school-age Ptarmigan cross the road?
His Ptarm Paper was due.

Why did the chicken cross the Baked Alaska?
There's just snow accounting for taste.

Why did the Eskimo Poet cross the road less-traveled?
To get away from all of the FROST around.

Why did the Snow Goose cross the road?
He was determined to get into Snow Business.

"...AND HOW ABOUT "GANDER," MY TOWN IN NEWFOUNDLAND, CANADA?"

"...MY KIND'A TOWN--"

Chicken, Alaska. *Approx.90 miles from Dawson City. Interesting remnants of old trading post. Got its name, they say, because miners who wanted to call it "ptarmigan" weren't sure of the spelling. "Chicken" is a nice name, too.*

How was the lame duck hurt?
> *She had a ding in her wing. An old mallard-y*
> *caused by fowl play in a Duck Blind.*

What do you call a duck in sweater-making class?
> *A Knitting Duck.*

What do you call a duck at seamstress school?
> *A Fitting Duck.*

Why does a goose go see a lawyer?
> *To prepare her last quill and testament.*

Why does a duck go to a lawyer?
> *To prepare her last bill and testament.*

Why did the duck cross the road?
> *To get to the other car pool.*

Pages from the

Len Hen

(Zen Master)

K.C. Jones

(Chicken Colonel)

Longa Luxian

(Lo-o-o-ng Island Duckling)

Family Album

Sir Francis Drake
(Chicken Explorer)

Pied Peeper
(Family Secret)

Crow Louis
(Boxer, Bantam Weight Division)

Newspaper article about gun-toting chickens:
Fowling piece.

Name a movie studio that makes fowl movies.
Metro-Golden-Fryer.

Formal dance for Chickens, Turkeys and Ducks:
Fowl Ball.

The chicken's two favorite authors:
John Fowles and Gene Fowler.

What are rural hens commonly called?
Yolk folk.

What organization do young chickens belong to?
The Fryer's Club.

What do ducks eat for breakfast?
A peeping-hot bowl of Quacker Oats.

Who are the turkey's favorite movie stars?
Clark Gobble and Betty Gobble.

Name the turkey's favorite novel.
"The House of Seven Gobbles."

What do turkeys eat at a baseball game?
Gobbler goobers.

What is a turkey's favorite stage play?
Hedda Gobbler.

What's the walkway in front of the turkey house paved with?
Gobble stones.

A favorite barnyard dessert:
Turkey cobbler.

Who repairs a turkey's shoes?
A Gobbler Cobbler.

Ill fowl:
    Sick chick

Fowl who drink a lot:
    Guzzling Goslings

Famous Fowl Singer:
    Alfred Drake

Famous science fiction hero:
    Duck Rogers

Crime against fowl:
    Geese Fleece

Popular candy for young fowl:
    Geese's Pieces

Famous Writers:
    * *Pearl Duck*
    * *Charles Chickens*
    * *Claire Booth Goose*

Famous Performers:
    * *Slim Chickens*
    * *Lee J. Squab*
    * *Goldie Swan*

Famous Rock and Roll Singer:
    Billy Swan

Driving chickens to market:
Cackle drive

Charity Chicken Organization:
Hens Across The Sea

Fowl jewelry:
Squabble Bauble

Chicken motto:
"Frica-see no evil"

Fowl food:
Corn on the squab

What do you call a group of unruly fowl?
Squab Mob

Young fowl queen:
Reign chick.

When does a duck hide?
During an earth-quack.

A group of religious ducks:
Quackers.

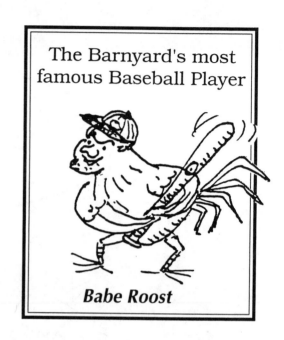

The Barnyard's most famous Baseball Player

Babe Roost

Fowl Telegram:
A chicken wire.

Person who promotes raising chickens:
Rooster Booster.

List of male chickens:
Rooster Roster.

Popular duck song:
  "A Pretty Girl is Like a Mallard-y."

U.S. President with lots of taste:
  Mallard Fillmore.

Fowl song:
  Mallard Ballad.

Baking competition for male ducks:
  The National Drake-Off

Served for fowl dinner:
  Mallard salad with Drake Steak.

When a male duck dies:
  Relatives hold a drake wake.

Fowl's favorite standup comedian:
  Richard Fryer.

A fowl who drinks:
  A Rum Cluck.

A fowl who never talks:
  Mum Cluck.

A fowl street-person.
  A Bum Cluck.

A depressed fowl:
  A Glum Cluck.

A fowl who forgot the words to the song:
  A Hum Cluck.

World's Fiercest Chicken
Attila the Hen!

Skinny Turkey:
   Paltry Poultry.

Car for male chickens:
   Rooster Roadster

Barnyard cookies:
   Graham Quackers.

The ghost of a chicken is called:
   A Poultry-geist.

Where do male chickens come from?
   Rooster, Massachusetts.

Movie about poultry.
   Chick flick.

Who is a chicken's favorite ice skater?
   Sonia Hen.
   (Ask your parents.)

Smart ducks are Wise Quacks.

What do baby chickens chew on?
   Chicklettes.

Fowl ice cream:
   Flocky road.

What ship takes chickens on a cruise?
　　A chicken sloop.

What do chickens pour on their feed to add zest?
　　Roostershire Sauce.

Male goose who works on railroad:
　　Gander dancer.

The Easter Bunny is . . .
　　an EGG-omaniac.

*"Good thing we're wearing
our Fowl Weather Gear."*

Fowl dessert:
   Drake cake.

Duck decoy:
   Fake Drake.

Where do you find fowl?
   In a Drake lake.

What does a fowl eat?
   Drake steak.

When a duck dies...
   They hold a Drake wake.

The Duck Who Forgot To

When two geese stop fighting:
   They declare a goose truce.

When all of the geese stop fighting:
   We have geese peace.

How did the wooden duck decoy cross the road?
   He lumbered across.

Why did the geese cross the lake in pairs?
   It was a two-for-one sail.

What does a chicken use to color her feathers?
Hen-na rinse.

What does a chicken use to write with?
A Hen pen.

A turkey with a foot injury?
A gobble with a hobble.

A turkey who drank too much:
A gobble with a wobble.

What do young Turkeys dress up like for Halloween?
Gobble-ins.

What do you use to re-start a tired rooster?
ROOSTER CABLES.

Weather-proof clothes for owls:
Owl Feather Gear.

A facial characteristic of fat Turkeys:
Fowl Jowls.

Chicken little is a FALL Guy!

What do chickens eat for breakfast?
Kellogg's Corn Flocks.

Fight in the barnyard:
Fowl brawl.

Screaming chickens.
Fowl Howl.

Popular board game for hens:
Chinese Chickers.

Chic Definitions...

Camera for fowl:
Chick click.

Unsophisticated chicken:
Hick chick.

Makeup for female fowl:
Chick stick.

Fowl with bad cold:
Sick chick.

Building material for chicken coops:
Chick bricks.

Chicken's favorite ball point pen:
Chick Bic.

Fowl who checks hats and coats:
Hat chick.

What Do You call. . .

Antelope that like stormy weather:
Fowl weather deer.

The drink chickens prefer during a storm:
Fowl weather beer.

The refuge chickens seek during a storm:
Fowl weather pier.

A fowl who keeps to herself:
Recluse goose.

Raised areas across barnyard roads:
Goose bumps.

The famous book by Mark Twain:
Duckleberry Finn.

What prompted the Rhode Island Red to cross the road?
She was in an agitated STATE of mind.

Male turkey who spies on people: *Peeping Tom.*

Duck who spies on people: *Peking Tom*

Small chick: *Peep Squeek.*

Chicken burlesque: *Peep Show.*

Math Proverb: Slow fowl + Busy road = *Squab Blob.*

Fowl tennis shot: *Squab Lob.*   Barnyard meter maid: *Chalk Chick.*

Fowl movie star: *Squab Throb.*   Barnyard movies: *Chick Flics.*

Fowl seafood: *Squab Squid.*   Fowl food: *Corn on the Squab.*

Why can't we fly an "X" or a "Y" for a change?

When rooster gangs fight what do they give each other:
   Flock Socks.

What's used to secure the chicken coop?   Goose bumps:
   Flock Locks.   *Flock Pocks.*

What's used to wake up the chickens?   Chicken-cooking pot:
   A Flock Clock.   *Flock Wok.*

How do you invest in chicken companies?   Chicken jokes:
   Buy Flock Stocks.   *Flock Yocks.*

Religious Fowl:
   Fryer Prior.

"That's Brother Chanticleer. He was the prior Friar."

"DAFFY-NOTIONS"

Songs passed on from chicken to chicken:
   Yolk songs.

Chickens' favorite dessert:
   Lay-er cake.

Thug chicken:
   Lays only hard-boiled eggs.

Planned Parenthood for chickens:
   The lay-away plan.

Chicken art:
   Hen scratchings.

Store where Fowl can hock items:
   Swan Shop.

Inebriated bird:
   Wobbly warbler.

Store where shrimp pawn things:
   Prawn Shop.

Chicken tradesman:
   Brick layer.

Fowl's rental agreement:
    Geese Lease.

Fowl relative:
    Geese Niece.

Opposite of Hawks:
    Peace Geese.

Duck who is a speed reader:
    Quick Quack.

Lousy worker in the barnyard:
    Cluck-Watcher.

A fowl good at math:
    Sum Kluck

Unclothed Fowl: *Stork naked.*

Financial Investments: *Storks and bonds.*

Small store owner: *Stork-keeper.*

Popular canned food: *Stork and beans.*

Best-loved Swan Songs: *"Swan-derful". . ."Swan-Knee, How I Love ya". . ."Swan Flew Over The Coo-koo's Nest."*

Why did the chicken ride the Lone Ranger's horse across his date farm in the desert?
> *He always wanted to cross his Palms with Silver.*

What happened to the Chipmonk when he crossed the busy road?
> *He was chip-wrecked.*

What does a crane like on his strawberry shortcake?
> *Whoop-ing cream.*

Why are Flamingos so healthy?
> *They're always in the pink of condition.*

What kind of breakfast is made with chicken wings?
> *Flap Jacks?*

What do you call a slow-moving Turkey on Thanksgiving?
> *Dinner.*

mother and Child

SECTION 3

REVEALED:

Notorious Egghead riddled with doubt.

Exclusive Interview Tells What Happened:

Reporter: Why did Humpty Dumpty cross the road?

First witness: *To tell Mother Goose about his accident.*

2nd. witness: *To make an accident report.*

King's Man: *To pull himself together!*

Reporter: What happened when H. D. fell off the wall?

King's Horse: *He was shell-shocked.*

King's Chef: *He insisted on scrambling back up.*

Reporter: What happened when H.D. fell off the wall into a kettle?

King's Other Horse: *He was boiling mad.*

No, you can't play football!
A Gridiron is no place for the likes of us!

What happened when Humpty Dumpty tripped on Times Square?
He made a big splash on Broadway.

Where is Humpty Dumpty considered a local hero?
In the Sandwich Islands.

When Humpty Dumpty fell off the wall, how did Mother Goose react?
She took it with a grain of salt.

Where did Humpty Dumpty land?
In a Humpty Dumpster!

Why was Humpty Dumpty on the wall in the first place?
Because he was- let's face it- a wall flower.

What is Humpty Dumpty's favorite store?
Wall Mart.

Why did Humpty Dumpty take the plunge?
His friends egged him on.

What did the pyschiatrist tell Humpty Dumpty?
He had a split personality.

Humpty Dumpty's favorite song:
"Breaking Up is Hard To Do."

Humpty Dumpty had a great fall... but a lousy Winter.

Why was Humpty Dumpty such a great audience?
He was so easy to break up!

How come Humpty Dumpty's friends called him "yellow"?
When he fell into trouble, he ran and ended up with egg on his face.

Why did Humpty Dumpty roll down the street?
He realized he was over the hill.

Why did Humpty Dumpty cross the road?
He was just out for a little roll.

Son, here's a bit of advice from my hero, Stonewall Jackson:
"It's not just lonely at the top— It's downright dangerous!"

"What happened to Humpty Dumpty when he fell?"
   "Nothing. He was much to shy to come out of his shell."

"Are you sure nothing happened to Humpty Dumpty?"
   "Well...he did seem kinda' shell-shocked."

"And was that the sum-total of it?"
   *"No. He went absolutely bonkers. Literally
   cracked under the strain."*

"There's more, isn't there?"
   *"Yes. First, all the King's Men just horsed around. Then, when
   Humpty Dumpty went to pieces, he was diagnosed as having a
   split personality."*

"Too bad. I always considered him a good egg. A real Cracker Jack"
   *"Me too. Don't repeat it, but I heard that Mother Goose
   set him up to be the fall guy."*

"SO YOU DECIDED TO TAKE A WALK. WHO EGGED YOU ON?"

Why does a Hard-boiled egg cross the road?
   To let off steam.

Recognize *L'eggs Benedict?*

How did the soft-boiled egg cross the road?
   He ran.

When was the soft-boiled egg unable to cross the road?
   He was arrested for poaching!

When does a hard-boiled egg cross the road?
   When he's boiling mad.

Where does a *really* hard-boiled egg cross the road?
   <u>*ANY WHERE*</u> *he wants to!*

Why did the soft-boiled egg decide not to cross the road?
   He preferred just to sit on his front poach.

When does a grilled egg cross the road?
   How about: "Only on FRIED day."

Where did the Deviled Egg cross the road?
    When he reached a pitch-fork in the road.

Why did the Deviled Egg cross the road?
    Just for the hell of it.

Why did the Easter Bunny keep crossing the road?
    He was a basket case.

Why did the chicken not cross the cotton field?
    She hemmed and hawed, then decided to skirt the area.

When did the rooster cross the bog?
    When he came to a Spring Chicken.

How did the spring chicken cross the road?
    She bounced.

Why did the redundant chicken always cross the road twice?
    She was double-jaunted.

She's a good mom...prepares all her kids' meals from scratch.

"An Interview With Sol. . ."

"Why did the Lumberjack cross the road"?
   "I don't know. You've stumped me."

"Well then, why did the Stone Mason cross the road?"
   "M-M-M-M-M. I'm in a quandry on that one."

"Let's give it another try: 'Why did the Lumberjack cross the road?'"
   "That is still a knotty question."

"Okay. Why did the Doctor cross the road?"
   "Maybe he was sick of all your questions."

"Back to basics: Why did the Chicken <u>keep crossing</u> the road?"
   "Would you repeat the question?"

"So why did the Stool Pigeon cross the road?"
   "I'll never tell!"

"This is your last chance: Why did the Invisible Man cross the road?"
   "Who?"

#

SECTION 4

THE CROSS-OVER SYNDROME:
Today's popular getaway

"BYE!"

Why did the copycat cross the road?
He was duped!

Where do fish cross the road?
At the School Crossing Sign.

How do Mermaids cross the road?
In a car pool.

And where do they cross?
In Fin-land.

Why did the DOGwood tree cross the road?
He was chasing a PUSSYwillow.

Why did the rattlesnake cross the road?
To get to the other sidewinder.

Why did the lion cross the road?
To get to the other pride.

Why did the detective
cross the road?

*Beats me.
I haven't a clue.*

Why did the groom cross the road?
To get to the other bride.

Why did the blackmailer cross the road?
To get to the other bribe.

Why did the trapper cross the road?
To get to the other hide.

Why did the hunter cross the road?
To get to the other side arm.

Why did the farmer cross the road?
To get to the other sod.

Why did the Chinese Chef cross the road?
*He just went for a **wok**.*

Why did the "Cow Girl" cross the road?
To get to the other side-saddle.

How did the frog cross the road?
He was toad across.

What railroad train only carries roosters?
The ones on spur lines.

How did the Trumpeter Swan cross the road?
He tootled across.

How did the Fried Egg cross the road?
He went over easy.

Why did the oilfield worker cross the road?
He felt his job was boring.

How do timber wolves cross the road?
In a splinter group, of course.

What did the baby whale do when he couldn't cross the road?
He sat down and blubbered.

Why did Lassie decide not to cross the road?
Poor thing was dog-tired.

What type of books do owls love to read?
WHOO-OO-Done-Its, of course.

Why did the cook have to leave?
He had a fryer engagement.

Why did the baker cross the berry patch?
It was a strawberry shortcut.

Famous Porcupine Humorist:
Q-will Rogers.

Why did the porcupine cross the road?
To get away from the sticks.

Why did the musician NOT cross the road?
He just couldn't face the music.

Why did the drummer cross the road?
To get to the other side-men and join the traffic jam.

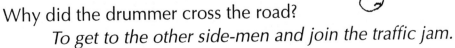

Why did the Doctor cross the road?
To get to the other bed-side.

Why did the race car driver cross the road?
To get to the in-side lane.

Why did the reporter ask the chicken: "Why did you cross the road?"
To get the inside story.

Why did the Dermatologist cross the road?
To treat the highway's bad case of Speed Bumps.

Why didn't the chicken cross the road?
Wasn't able to get out of a fryer engagement.

Where does the Swallow cross the river?
At its mouth.

When does Father Time cross the road?
Whenever he gets ticked off.

How can you tell when a chicken is angry?
    By his Fowl Scowl.

What was the little-known period in China's history when
             young geese ruled the land:
    The Gos-LING Dynasty.

Name the Australian fowl with a pouch to carry an extra comb.
    The Kanga-Rooster.

A sure tip-off to a very sleepy fowl:
    Swan yawns.

Where did the cook work while crossing the range?
    In the Chick Wagon.

When did the chicken doublecross the Survey-Taker?
    After she came to her census.

When did the electrician fowl up?
    When he got his chicken wires crossed.

Why did the Chick Pea cross the road?
He had four very good reasons:
* he hadn't BEAN there for while.
* it was time to split.
* he didn't want to vegetate.
* he was "garden" the area.

When did the chick pea cross the road?
During a pea-soup fog.

Spending Quality Time With the Children

Out for an Egg Roll

Why did the chicken cross the Gazebo?
"The What?"
"Gazebo!"
"Gesundheit!"

Why does a flock of geese always fly in a "V"?
They can't afford a Cadillac.

How did the Rooster help Moses?
He parted the Red Sea with his comb.

What happened when the cucumber crossed the busy road?
He got into a pickle. (And it was SO cucumbersome!)

What happened to the gooseberries crossing a busy highway?
They got themselves into a jam.

Who crosses the street before the Jay?
"I" does.

Why did the Mandarin Duck meander across the junk yard?
She wanted to buy a Chinese sailboat.

Way To Go!

When do rodents cross the road?
Only when they have the "rat of way."

How about birds?
When they have the Flight of way.

And Dragons?
When they have the Fright of way.

Okay, then where does King Arthur cross the road?
At the Knight of way.

Great! Then of course authors would cross the road...
At the Write of way.

Now try this one: When did Little Miss Muffet cross the road?
When she had the right of Whey.

And, why did Wilbur and Orville cross the road without hesitation.
They knew they had the Wright of way.

It's understood that the Army crosses the road with impudence. Why???
They know they possess the Might of way.

Where did the engaged couple cross the road?
Where the sign said, "Merge."

When does the baseball pitcher cross the road?
When the light says "balk."

How can you tell the friendly duck?
He's the one always ready to quack a smile.

Why did the chicken cross the Blue Danube?
Seems he was in a black mood and wanted to paint the town red.

Where did the ram cross the road?
When he reached the a-BUTT-ment.

Why did the Anesthesiologist cross the operating room?
To get to the Ether side.

When did the Cowardly Lion cross the road to OZ?
Only when the light turned yellow.

Why did the Toe Truck cross the road?
To get to the foot-hills.

Why did the Teamster cross the road?
He didn't want to have any truck with chickens.

How did the Top Sergeant cross the river?
He barged across.

Why did the Road Hog cross the road?
To get to the Porking Lot.

Why did the Rabbi at Passover cross the temple?
To get to the other Seder.

Why did the chicken cross the forest?
To get to the other Cedar.

Why did Ronald McDonald cross the road?
To get to the other side of fries.

Taking Sides...

Why did the trapper cross the road?
To get to the Otter side.

Why did the incoherent chicken cross the road?
To get to the Mutter side.

Why did the dairy farmer cross the road?
To get to the Butter side.

Why did the tailor cross the road?
To get to the Cutter side.

Why did the bowler cross the alley?
To get to the Gutter side.

Why did the golfer cross the road?
To get to the Putter side.

Why did the sailor cross the road?
To get to the Rudder side.

Why did the speech therapist cross the road?
To get to the Stutter side.

Why did father cross the road?
To get to Mother's side.

Why did the young girl cross the road?
To get to her Brother's side.

How did the CARTOONIST cross the strip?

He soared across in a BALLOON!

In Tribute to:

HARRY S. STEWMAN

Distinguished Pullet-ician

Why did the Publisher cross the road?
To get to the Author side.

Why did "Mr. Clean" cross the road?
To get to the Odor side.

Why did the Complaint Manager cross the room?
To get to the Over-sight.

Why did the Gym Teacher cross the class?
To get to the Over-sized.

Why did the Cleaning Lady cross the teenager's room?
To get to the Clutter Side.

Why did the Farmer's Wife cross the chicken coop?
To get to the Flutter Side.

Why did the Logger cross the road?
To get to the Wood-side.

Why did the Chickory cross the road?
To get to the coffee grounds.

Why did the chicken cross the snow bank?
To deposit his chicken feed.

Why did the chicken cross the Ski Lodge?
She decided to "Ski for herself."

Why did the duck cross the Ski Lodge?
Poor thing was "Ski sick."

When did the AArdvark cross the road?
When the light said"Vark."

How did the daring stork cross the road?
Stork naked!

What fowl never crosses the road?
A Sitting Duck.

Why was the chicken walking round and round the IRS Building?
Her accountant told her she had to take a Tax Hike.

How come the chicken couldn't get across Silicon Valley?
Too much Computer Traffic.

Why did the Rhodes Scholar not cross Turkey?
He had forgotten to book passage.

Why did the prospector cross the Mother Lode country?
He wanted to change his mine.

Why did the prospector NOT cross the Mother Lode country?
He changed his mind about changing his mine.

Why did the road cross the lettuce patch?
Simply a case of Imminent Romaine.

Just how did the chicken cross the Great Divide?
She split.

How was the chicken able to slide across Greece so easily?
She was a "slick" chick.

Where did the hearse cross the road?
> *When it came to a dead end.*

When did the Proctologist cross the road?
> *When he came to a dead end.*

Where did Rumplestilskin cross the road?
> *When he came to the Troll Bridge.*

Why did the romantic young maiden cross the road?
> *To get to the other sigh.*

Why did the barber cross the road?
> *To get to the other sideburn.*

Was the computer nerd able to cross the Information Superhighway?
> *Yes, but it was a Hard Drive.*

Why did the nest egg cross the road?
> *To open a <u>branch</u> office.*

INCUBATION
IS A HENS-ON OPERATION

Why did Peter Piper cross the road?
To get out of the pickle he was in.

Why did the crab cross the enchanted forest?
To play Dungeness and Dragons.

How did the ram cross the road?
He made a EWE turn.

What's it called when ghosts raid the hen house?
A Poultry-heist.

Why did the Wild Goose cross the busy dangerous road?
Hey, they don't call him 'wild' for nothing.

Why did the hunter cross the marshes?
It was a wild goose chase.

Why did the Road Runner cross the road?
To get to the other cartoon.

And just how did the Road Runner cross the road?
In a very animated manner.

How did the penguin cross the road?
He had to go with the floe.

Why did the stallion cross the road?
He was just horsing around.

Why did the chicken cross the horse breeder's ranch?
To get to the other sire.

Why did the chicken soup cross the road?
To get to the other Jewish Mother.

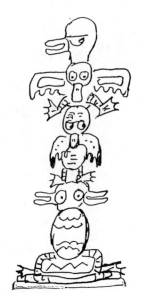

How did the wild duck cross Colorado?
She made a Boulder dash.

Why did the duck cross the Indian Reservation?
To get to the other Sioux.

PLAYING "CHICKEN"

How was the chicken able to cross Ireland so fast?
She did it in Dublin time.

Why didn't the army tank cross the road?
It got side-tracked.

Why did the pharmacist cross the lab?
To get to the side effects.

Why did the calf NOT cross the theater?
She just didn't heifer act together.

Why did the crab cross the courtroom?
He had Just Claws to do so.

Why does a Turkey hate Thanksgiving?
Because that is when his goose is cooked.

"Why did the Doctor cross the road?"
I'm sick of your questions.

I repeat: "Why did the Doctor cross the road?"
You know, you're taxing my patients!

Well then, "Why did the IRS Collector cross the road?"
Now, you're really taxing my patience!

"Why did the schizophrenic cross the road?"
I don't know...but here he comes again!

Squab Job 1:
CROSS THAT ROAD!

"— AND ONE FOR THE ROAD."

Why did the Road Warrier cross the road?
To get to the Gas War.

Why did the Librarian cross the road?
Shhh...not so loud.

Why did the Proctologist cross the road?
That's just the way he was reared.

Why did the Semanticist cross the road?
Are you speaking literally or metaphorically?

Why did the Philosopher cross the road?
Would you please define "cross" and "road"?

Why did the Psychologist cross the road?
Just one of the detours we all take in a lifetime.

Why did the Hustler cross the road?
Give me a buck and I'll tell you.

Definition: Comforter Confusion=
Goose Down fowl-up.

What did Goose Down do when the air raid started?
He took cover in his "comforter zone."

Why did the feather pillow cross the road?
To get to the road bed.

How did the fox feel after raiding the goose pen?
He felt a little down in the mouth.

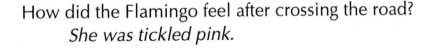

What Holiday is widely celebrated by Roosters?
Feather's Day!

How did the Flamingo feel after crossing the road?
She was tickled pink.

What kind of Fowl-Weather Gear is useful in rain and snow?
Duck-A-Lucks.

Name a popular entertainment couple:
Hugh and Goose Downs.

How do you spoil a new egg?
By coddling it.

How do poultry farmers seal a business deal?
With a warm HEN SHAKE.

What does a wet hen wear to official occasions?
A formal Wet Suit.

Why did the chicken cross the Greek Island?
To get to the sunny side of Crete.

How did the farmer provide for all of the extra chicks?
He added another wing to his chicken coop.

*If a duck's final song is a Mallard Ballad,
wouldn't a Cygnet sing a Swan Song?*

A Little Light Lamp-oonery

Why did the Goose-necked Lamp NOT cross the road?

she just didn't want to stick her neck out, or...
she couldn't make connections, or...
she couldn't see the light.

Why did the Goose-necked lamp decide to cross the road?

she thought it was a bright idea, or...
she was all wired up, or...
she was aglow with anticipation, or...
she was burning with curiosity.

How did the carpenter cross the road?
He lumbered across.

Why did the lumberjack cross the road?
He had an axe to grind.

Why didn't the optometrist cross the road?
He refused to make a spectacle of himself.

Why did Anold Palmer cross the road?
He was only playing a round.

Why did the golfer refuse to cross the road?
He was just tee-d off.

Why did the midget cross the road?
He was taking a short cut.

Why did the butcher cross the road?
He decided to take a short "cut."

Why did Jack Frost NOT cross the windy street?
He was a confirmed draft dodger.

Why did Jack Frost NOT cross the mountain?
He just couldn't climate.

Why did the Canadian Goose cross the road?
He was determined to bring home the bacon.

Why did Jack-Be-Nimble cross the road?
It was Leap Year.

Where did Jack-Be-Nimble decide to cross the road?
At Candlestick Park, naturally.

Why did the Ugly Duckling cross the road?
Who cares. I'm just glad it's gone!

HONK If you dig wild geese!

Why did the nature photographer cross the road?
To get to the Otter side.

Why did Tommy Smothers cross the road?
To get to his brother's side.

Why did the Kissing Bandit cross the road?
To get to the side of Law and Ardor.

Why did the rifleman cross the road?
To get to the other side-arm.

Why did the pyschologist cross the road?
To get to the insight.

Why did the tourist cross the road?
To get to the inn side.

Why did Father Time cross the road
back & forth...back & forth?
Result of his nervous tick.

Why was the Colossus of Rhodes unable to cross Greece?
He was bound not to, being a Statue of Limitations.

If that's the case, how <u>did</u> the Colossus of Rhodes manage to cross Greece?
This Statue of Limitations simply ran out.

What road do depressed chickens take?
The Low Road

How do Fruit Flies cross the road?
A group effort. Always in PEARS.

Why did the Dove cross the road?
Just to find some peace.

Why did the Hawk cross the road?
To get to the other war.

Why did the photographer cross the road?
To get to the other slide show.

What road do alcoholic crabs take?
The high road...leading to the nearest sand Bar.

Why did the cow cross the road?
To get to the Udder side.

Why did the hog insist on crossing the street against heavy traffic?
   He was dumb and pig-headed.

How did the flea escape across the road?
   He decided to take it on the lamb.

Why did the couch potato cross the road?
   He went off half-baked.

Why did the chicken just sit and stew all day?
   You think her life was all gravy?

Why did the pachyderm cross the road?
   She was searching for a spot to un-pack her derm.

Why didn't the obedient chicken cross the rope bridge?
   A. *Her mother told her knot to, and,*
   B. *She was "frayed" to disobey.*

Why did the chicken cross the mole hill?
   Because her troubles were "mountain" daily.

"Side Affects"

Why did the disc jockey cross the recording studio?
To get to the flip side.

Why did the acrobat cross the circus?
To get to the flip side.

Why did the lumberjack cross the road?
To get to the wood-side.

Why did the surveyor cross the road?
To get to the other site.

Why did the lawyer cross the funeral hall?
To get to the other scion.

Why did the waitress cross the roadhouse?
To get to the other side dish.

Chicken on the Menu

Why did the Lemon Chicken NOT cross the road?
Couldn't. Poor thing was plumb puckered out.

Why did the Duck a l'Orange cross the road?
Because it was so a-peeling.

Why did the Chicken Kiev cross the road?
To join the Communist Pot.

Why did the Chicken Salad NOT cross the road?
She couldn't sandwich it in.

Why did the Chicken Liver cross the road?
To join the onions.

Why did the chicken carry a load of junk across the road?
To get to the Dump-ling grounds.

Why did the Chicken Cacciatore cross the road?
To give the Chef a Pizza her mind.

A Little "Light Reading"

Where did the chicken cross the Flea Market?

At the swap light.

Where did the salesman cross the road?
At the shop light.

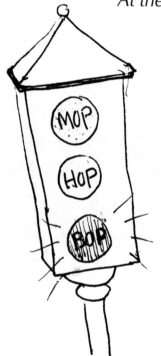

Where did the maid cross the road?
At the mop light.

Where did the kangaroo cross the road?
At the hop light.

Where does the jazz muscian cross the road?
At the bop light.

Where did the tea salesman cross the road?
At the STEEP sign.

Where does the policeman cross the road?
At the cop light.

Where does the parachutist cross the road?
At the drop light.

Where does the play producer cross the road?
At the flop light.

Where does the sponge diver cross the road?
At the sop light.

Riddled with Rhymes

When do the baby chicks cross the road?   *During peep year.*

Why did Antelope cross the road?   *It was leap year.*

Why do snails cross the road?   *It was c-r-e-e-p year.*

When do old cars cross the road to the junk yard?   *During heap year.*

When do housekeepers cross the road?   *During sweep year.*

When do wheat farmers cross the road?   *During reap year.*

When do plumbers cross the road?   *During seep year.*

When do mountain climbers cross the road?   *During steep year.*

And what about censors?   *Bleep year.*
And musicians?   *Beep year.*
And swimmers?   *During lap year.*
And the drunkards?   *Loop year.*

And when do horses cross the road?
During lope year.

Why did the Shriner get angry after crossing the hen house?
Because he ended up with egg on his fez.

And why did the dainty lady crossing the hen house also become upset.
She, as expected, got egg on her lace.

Why was the cowboy mad while driving his cattle across the barnyard?
He got egg on his steer.

Why did the Mortician get mad after detouring through the henhouse?
Because he ended up with egg in his bier.

What would you call a weird chicken that lays strange shaped eggs?

Egg-centric

Why did the bald eagle cross the road?
   To have a hair-raising adventure.

Why did the bald eagle get married?
   To have a heir raising adventure.

Why did the wet hen hesitate to cross the pond?
   She wavered, not having brought her water wings.

What did Henny Penny get for crossing the road?
   She got a run for her money.

Why were the dumplings afraid to cross the border?
   They were chicken and didn't want a ticket for "illegal dumpling".

When did Charlie the Tuna cross the road by the sea?
   After he tide one on.

Why did Charlie <u>not</u> cross the road?
   It was beyond his beach.

"CHICKEN OF THE SEA"

Visiting Fowl from Around the World

- Ducks from "Ducksenburg"
- A Rooster from Wooster
- Swan from Bonn
- Crane from the Ukraine
- Stork from County Cork
- Drake from Wake Island
- Egg Foo Yung from "Yolk-ahama"

*Featuring Games for
Every Age & Persuasion*

- *Mumblety Egg*
- *Wild Goose Chase*
- *Deluxe Crow-Quet,*
  Featuring Wooden Mallards
- *The Ole Shell Game*
- *Wing Toss*

Why did the chicken cross the wedding chapel?
   To get to the other bride.

Why did the Rooster cross the fruit orchard?
   He was a peach comber.

Why did the chicken cross the detective agency?
   He wanted to get down to cases.

Why did the chicken cross the wine warehouse?
   To get down to cases.

Why didn't the inchworm cross the flagpole?
   He just couldn't "measure up."

When did the fowl cross the recruiting office?
   When he was in-DUCK-ted into the army.

Why did the Rhode Island Red Chicken cross the cemetary?
   To get to the Communist PLOT.

"It's Spring-Time in the Yockies"

Where did the rooster cross the stream?
When he came to a "Spring" Chicken.

How did the spring chicken cross the road?
She bounced.

What happened when the Spring chicken tried to cross the road?
The Spring chicken had a bad Fall.

When did the Spring Chicken cross the road?
Only after she got all wound up.

What prompted the Spring Chicken to cross the road?
She was bounced from her job.

What happened when the Spring Chicken attempted to cross the road?
She went wound and wound in circles.

How did the Spring Chicken cross the road?
Possibly on a Pogo Stick.

What do you have when a goose takes to the air?
A fowl up.

What do you have when a goose goes outside?
You have a fowl out.

What do you call an establishment for chickens and geese
to eat and sleep for a night?
A Fowl Inn.

Why did the chicken stay in the center of the road?
She was ambivalent and couldn't take either side.

Why did the bull keep crossing from one side of the road to the other?
He was <u>steer</u> crazy.

Why did the hen's teeth cross the road?
They were told to make themselves scarce.

Why did the mime cross the road?
How should I know...do I look like a mime reader?

Unpleasant Pheasant

Clock Cock

Lickin' Chickin'

Why did the chicken refuse to have dinner in Petaluma?
She discovered she was the main course.

How did the mother hen get her brood across Petaluma?
On a bike: she pedaled her peepers.

How did the clever chicken cross Petaluma?
Incognito.

What kind of pullman car did she use when crossing?
One with a very wide berth.

What did Petaluma citizens plan for Mother Goose when she
came to visit?
A cook's tour.

And how were they going to spice up her tour?
With salt, pepper and Oregano for sure.

So why did Mother Goose <u>not</u> cross Petaluma?
She'd already crossed it off her list.

Jerky Turkey   **Mucky Ducky**   **Moose Goose**

Where does a lame duck go to cross the road?
   To the Hospital Zone.

Why did Winchester, Colt and Remington run across the road?
   It was another Arms Race.

When do plasterers cross the road?
   Whenever their LATHS cross.

When did the soprano cross the road?
   When she came to a tuning <u>fork</u> in the road.

Why didn't the frozen chicken cross the road?
   He was scared stiff.

When did Mark Twain cross the road?
   Only during in-Clement weather.

Why do geese fly south during the winter?
   No $$$ to catch the train.

DUCKS IN A ROW

Where do storks come from in Russia?
   The U-crane.

If chickens get Chicken Pox and geese get Goose Bumps,
what do Cranes get?
   Crane Sprain.

Why did the chicken cross the open road?
   To get to the other song.

What did the vegetarian do when he ran out of vegetables?
   He was forced to bite the pullet.

Why did the housewife cross the Fjord?
   To get to the iceberg lettuce.

How did the talking bird feel after safely fighting his way across
the road traffic?
   He said it was only a Mynah victory.

How did the swan know she was in Hollywood?
   She came to a Reel-Road crossing sign.

PEEKING DUCK

The End

ORDER FORM

Please send ____copies of *The World's Greatest Book of Chicken Jokes and Other Fowl Humor* ....@ *$9.95*

(Please include $2 shipping for the first book, 75¢ for each additional book.)

Sales Tax: *Add 8.25% for books shipped to a California address.*

Payment: _____Check.   _____Money Order.   _____Cash.

Ship to:

Name _____

Address _____Apt:._____

City_____State_____ Zip_____

Mail your order to: JESTER Books
3 Monte Vista Road
Orinda, CA 94563